Healthy Cooking For One

Quick and Easy Healthy Recipes from Breakfast to Dessert for Just You

Dereck Moore

All rights reserved © 2020 by Louise Davidson and The Cookbook Publisher. No part of this publication or the information in it may be quoted from or reproduced in any form by means such as printing, scanning, photocopying, or otherwise without prior written permission of the copyright holder.

This book is presented solely for motivational and informational purposes. The author and the publisher do not hold any responsibility for errors, omissions, or contrary interpretation of the subject matter herein.

The recipes provided in this book are for informational purposes only and are not intended to provide dietary advice. A medical practitioner should be consulted before making any changes in diet. Additionally, recipes' cooking times may require adjustment depending on the age and quality of appliances. Readers are strongly urged to take all precautions to ensure ingredients are fully cooked to avoid the dangers of foodborne illnesses. The recipes and suggestions provided in this book are solely the opinions of the author. The author and publisher do not take any responsibility for any consequences that may result due to following the instructions provided in this book.

All the nutritional information contained in this book is provided for informational purposes only. This information is based on the specific brands, ingredients, and measurements used to make the recipe, and therefore the nutritional information is an estimate, and in no way is intended to be a guarantee of the actual nutritional value of the recipe made in the reader's home. The author and the publisher will not be responsible for any damages resulting in your reliance on the nutritional information. The best method to obtain an accurate count of the nutritional value in the recipe is to calculate the information with your specific brands, ingredients, and measurements.

ISBN: 9798585305276

Printed in the United States

www.thecookbookpublisher.com

CONTENTS

INTRODUCTION 1

BREAKFAST 5

CHICKEN AND POULTRY 13

BEEF, PORK, LAMB AND VEAL 23

FISH AND SEAFOOD 37

VEGETARIAN 47

SNACKS AND SMALL BITES 59

DESSERTS 71

RECIPE INDEX 83

APPENDIX 87

INTRODUCTION

This cookbook is all about recipes that serve one portion with healthy, filling ingredients. If you were wondering whether cooking can be fun when you're cooking only for yourself, the answer is absolutely yes. It can be easy and fulfilling if you know the right tips and techniques, and if you don't know them already, I will share them with you in this introduction.

Let's all admit that the easiest thing is to order pizza or takeaway meals and feed ourselves with foods that, delicious as they may be, usually tend to be processed and not good for our bodies. While I was writing this cookbook, I was picking ingredients that are healthy and delicious *at the same time*—things that are good for our bodies. From delicious breakfasts with perfect nutritional values to meat recipes that are light and rich in Protein. Seafood will never be tastier than with these recipes presented in this book, and for all of my vegetarian readers out there, I have picked perfect meals for you that are filling and rich in nutrients. For savory and sweet snacks on a busy day, you will find perfect ideas that you can prepare in just five minutes. And for those who have a sweet tooth, you are going to love my avocado chocolate mousse and you won't taste the avocado at all!

If you are living in a hurry, one of the most important things to have in mind is the meal prepping your dishes. And this means it's very important to plan your shopping list. Some of the most common ingredients for living a healthy lifestyle are fresh veggies and fruits, eggs, Proteins coming from fish like salmon or shrimp, and some light cheeses like mozzarella, goat cheese, and feta. I would highly recommend shopping in the bulk bin aisle at the grocery store. By calculating exactly what you will need you won't waste money buying more, and you won't be left with open jars and packages cluttering up your kitchen cabinets while you wonder how to use them next. People always over-buy at the grocery store but remember that you are cooking for one, so don't buy too much. All you want to have is fresh ingredients in your meals; that's how nutrients are absorbed into your body. If you practice meal prepping so you already know what to buy at the grocery store, you can buy only what you need. Cooking for one can be easy and simple, and it has its own benefits. For example, you can cook what you crave at the moment and not compromise with other people's wishes and ideas. Another pro is that you can decide when to cook your meals. You can cook just before you leave for work, in your pajamas at night, or while you are listening to your favorite song or watching a TV show.

I'm a greedy eater, so even when I'm cooking for one, I always cook a little bit more than one serving, just in case I feel that I need more. But because you are cooking for one, you don't need a big pot to cook your small amount of pasta, or a big nonstick frying pan to cook a single-serving dish. If you feel that you can eat the same dish twice in a week, you can double the recipe and save time on your next lunch/dinner. If you find yourself with leftovers, you can totally use them up for your next cooking project. You can make canapes or bruschetta with the leftover food from breakfast and make easy, quick snacks for later. Most of the recipes travel well, so you can make them and bring them to your workplace, a friend's gathering, or wherever you go later in the day. If you want to be successful in cooking for one, you need to meal prep your meals because you will have the necessary ingredients in your pantry and you will be all set up to quickly cook the recipes that you will find in this cookbook.

Cooking for one doesn't have to be a pain and take a lot of time. When it comes to cooking family-friendly meals, or dinner recipes, families come out on top, but I have decided to present you with single-serving recipes. You will see that some desserts can be made in 5 minutes, using the microwave instead of baking them in the oven. You will love this cookbook when you see how easy it is to prepare your favorite snacks. All recipes require no more than 30–35 minutes in the kitchen, and most of them require no more than 20 minutes, so you are going to fall in love with this cookbook once you try out a recipe or two. If cooking for one was your challenge, you are now all ready to accept it and enjoy the journey. Whether you live alone or you are a parent who wants to indulge while your kids enjoy their own favorite meals (prepared as single servings) you will treasure this collection of foolproof recipes that will never fail you.

The number of single-person households in the U.S. is over 35 million, and it's growing every year. But cooking for one isn't just for people who live alone; it's also great if you have picky eaters in the family or a husband/wife who travels often. I am sure that with these recipes, you are going to make cooking more fun for yourself. Eating healthy means that you will have breakfast, lunch, dinner, and at least one snack/dessert a day.

BREAKFAST

Overnight Oats

Oats for breakfast can be an easy-to-make, make-ahead meal that will keep you full until lunchtime. There are many different ways to prepare oats with countless toppings to make every day more sensual than the last.

Prep time 5 minutes

Ingredients
½ cup whole rolled oats
½ cup almond milk
½ teaspoon honey
1 tablespoon Greek yogurt
1 teaspoon chia seeds
2 apricots, diced

Directions
1. In a large glass or serving bowl, mix the rolled oats with almond milk and honey.
2. Refrigerate for 30 minutes to overnight.
3. Just before serving, top with the Greek yogurt, chia seeds, and diced apricots.

Nutrition (per serving)
Calories 494, fat 35.8 g, carbs 38.4 g, sugar 14.7 g, Protein 12 g, sodium 36 mg

Breakfast Burrito

Are you running out of healthy breakfast ideas that will keep you energized for a long period of time? This breakfast burrito will take you only 15 minutes to make and will also be the best one you have tried for many years!

Prep time 5 minutes | Cooking time 10 minutes

Ingredients
1 teaspoon chipotle paste
1 large egg
1 teaspoon olive oil
1 cup kale
½ cup cherry tomatoes halved
½ small avocado, sliced
1 tortilla wrap, warmed

Directions
1. In a bowl, mix the egg with the chipotle paste.
2. Season with salt and pepper to taste.
3. Warm the olive oil in a nonstick frying pan over medium heat and add the kale and the cherry tomatoes.
4. Stir in the egg with the chipotle paste and cook until the omelet is cooked through.
5. Place the omelet on the warmed tortilla wrap and arrange the avocado slices.
6. Wrap tightly and serve.

Nutrition (per serving)
Calories 522, fat 33.3 g, carbs 45.5 g, sugar 5.6 g, Protein 15.3 g, sodium 569 mg

Banana Pancakes

Pancakes are the most popular American breakfast recipe that everyone worldwide enjoys in many different ways. I am sharing a foolproof recipe for banana pancakes that will make your morning so scrumptious you'll feel like you are eating in a fancy bar. If you put in a little extra effort and brew some espresso, you will enjoy this recipe the most.

Prep time 5 minutes | Cooking time 10 minutes

Ingredients
1 large egg
½ cup mashed banana (around 1 large banana)
2 tablespoons olive oil
1 teaspoon vanilla extract
⅓ cup almond milk
¾ cup whole wheat flour
¼ cup oat flour
1 teaspoon baking powder
½ teaspoon ground cinnamon
Pinch of nutmeg
1 tablespoon ground pecans
1 tablespoon maple syrup

Directions
1. In a large mixing bowl, mix the egg, mashed banana, olive oil, vanilla, and almond milk.
2. In another bowl, mix the whole wheat flour, oat flour, baking powder, ground cinnamon, nutmeg, and ground pecans.
3. Mix the dry ingredients into the wet ingredients until combined.
4. Warm a nonstick frying pan over medium heat and add dollops of batter to form the pancakes. Cook for about 1 minute on each side.

5. Serve on a plate, drizzled with maple syrup and topped with extra banana slices, if desired.

Nutrition (per serving)
Calories 1029, fat 48.5 g, carbs 127.9 g, sugar 27.1 g
Protein 24 g, sodium 112 mg

Mushroom and Herb Omelet

Do you think that an omelet needs to be complicated? I don't think so! Try out my foolproof recipe that doesn't require many ingredients but comes out perfect, just like the omelets you eat in a restaurant. This one is with mushrooms and different herbs, but you can always make your own version with the ingredients most available or most appealing to you at the moment.

Prep time 5 minutes | Cooking time 5 minutes

Ingredients
2 large eggs, lightly beaten
1 tablespoon sour cream
1 teaspoon chopped chives
1 teaspoon chopped basil
1 teaspoon chopped parsley
Salt and pepper to taste
1 cup diced mushrooms
1 teaspoon olive oil

Directions
1. Warm the olive oil on a nonstick frying pan over medium heat.
2. Add the diced mushrooms.
3. Season with salt and pepper to taste and stir in the chopped chives, parsley, and basil.
4. In another bowl, whisk the eggs and sour cream together. Pour over the herbs and mushrooms.
5. Cook, covered, for 5 minutes.

Nutrition (per serving)
Calories 225, fat 17.4 g, carbs 3.8 g, sugar 2 g, Protein 15.3 g, sodium 151 mg

Avocado Toast

Are you tired of the classic mashed avocado spread on a slice of bread? Then you are here at the right time! I am making a great avocado mash with seasonings to make it more delicious, and guess what? I am topping the whole thing with fresh feta cheese for a refreshing taste.

Prep time 5 minutes

Ingredients
2 slices wholewheat bread, toasted
1 avocado, mashed
¼ teaspoon garlic powder
Salt and pepper to taste
½ teaspoon dried oregano
½ teaspoon chili flakes
Juice of ½ lemon
3 ounces feta cheese, crumbled

Directions
1. In a medium mixing bowl, mash the avocado with a fork.
2. Season with salt and pepper to taste and the garlic powder, dried oregano, chili flakes, and lemon juice. Mix.
3. Spread the avocado spread on the toast.
4. Top with crumbled feta cheese and serve.

Nutrition (per serving)
Calories 778, fat 59.3 g, carbs 45 g, sugar 7.9 g
Protein 23.4 g, sodium 1226 mg

Smoothie Bowl

Smoothies can be made and eaten in a bowl as well. This is a great smoothie bowl recipe that will pack you with nutrients, Proteins, and vitamins to keep your healthy lifestyle in line. I love making it and topping it with different things like bananas, hazelnuts, and chia seeds.

Prep time 5 minutes

Ingredients
1 large banana, peeled
¾ cup almond milk
1 tablespoon peanut butter
½ teaspoon vanilla extract
1 teaspoon chia seeds
½ banana, peeled
3 tablespoons chopped hazelnuts

Directions
1. Place the banana, almond milk, peanut butter, and vanilla in a large mixing bowl.
2. Puree until creamy and thick.
3. Pour into a serving bowl and top with chia seeds, sliced banana, and chopped hazelnuts.
4. Serve immediately.

Nutrition (per serving)
Calories 792, fat 64.3 g, carbs 52.8 g, sugar 25 g
Protein 14 g, sodium 104 mg

CHICKEN AND POULTRY

Primavera Stuffed Chicken

This dish is anything but boring. It's juicy, full of flavor, and very presentable. The most important thing is that it's loaded with veggies and it's insanely good. You must try it to believe it.

Prep time 10 minutes | Cooking time 25 minutes

Ingredients
1 boneless skinless chicken breast
½ zucchini, cut into rounds
1 medium tomato, cut into rounds
1 yellow bell pepper, cut into strips
1 tablespoon olive oil
½ teaspoon Italian seasoning
Salt and pepper to taste
¼ cup shredded mozzarella cheese

Directions
1. Drizzle the olive oil in a heatproof baking dish.
2. Cut slits in the chicken and insert the sliced zucchini, tomato, and bell pepper therein.
3. Season with salt and pepper to taste and top with mozzarella.
4. Sprinkle with Italian seasoning and bake in a preheated oven at 350°F (180°C) for 20–25 minutes or until the chicken is cooked through.
5. Serve with a green salad.

Nutrition (per serving)
Calories 337, fat 19.2 g, carbs 17.6 g, sugar 11.1 g
Protein 26.7 g, sodium 113 mg

Perfectly Baked Chicken Breast

To be honest, the chicken breast tends to be bland, especially when it's skinless. But with this recipe, you are going to have nothing less than a juicy and flavorful piece of chicken on your plate.

Prep time 10 minutes | Cooking time 25 minutes

Ingredients
1 chicken breast, boneless and skinless
½ teaspoon dried paprika
½ teaspoon garlic powder
1 tablespoon honey
1 tablespoon olive oil
½ teaspoon Italian seasoning
Salt and pepper to taste
Juice and zest of 1 lemon

Directions
1. In a small bowl, combine the olive oil, honey, dried paprika, lemon juice and peel, garlic powder, and Italian seasoning.
2. Season the chicken breast with salt and pepper to taste and drizzle with the honey glaze.
3. Bake in a preheated oven at 350°F (180°C) for 20–25 minutes or until the chicken is cooked through. It will have a nice red color because of the paprika.
4. Serve with a green salad.

Nutrition (per serving)
Calories 330, fat 17.5 g, carbs 24.6 g, sugar 19.4 g
Protein 22.3 g, sodium 55 mg

Air Fryer Chicken Breast Recipe

When it comes to chicken recipes, we typically want to roast the chicken or deep fry it. Roasting is healthy, there's no doubt about that, but with modern technology why don't we go a level up and use an air fryer? It's quick, it's juicy and it's super delicious!

Prep time 10 minutes | Cooking time 15 minutes

Ingredients
1 large egg, room temperature
1 tablespoon cornflour
2 tablespoons breadcrumbs
1 tablespoon grated Parmesan cheese
½ teaspoon dried oregano
Salt and pepper to taste
1 boneless skinless chicken breast

Directions
1. Season the chicken breast with salt and pepper to taste.
2. In a bowl, whisk the egg with a fork.
3. Dip the chicken breast in the beaten egg.
4. In another bowl, combine the cornflour, breadcrumbs, Parmesan cheese, and dried oregano.
5. Coat the chicken breast with the dry ingredients and place it in an air fryer.
6. Cook for 15 minutes at 350°F (180°C).
7. Flip the chicken over and cook for 5 minutes more.
8. Serve with baby spinach.

Nutrition (per serving)
Calories 358, fat 14.6 g, carbs 17.3 g, sugar 1.3 g
Protein 38.9 g, sodium 480 mg

Lemon Garlic Baked Drumsticks

We often love chicken drumsticks only when they are attached to the whole chicken. But these individual lemon garlic baked drumsticks are delicious and easy to prepare. Soy sauce and lemon juice make all the difference in this recipe.

Prep time 10 minutes | Cooking time 25 minutes

Ingredients
2 chicken drumsticks
1 tablespoon low sodium soy sauce
1 tablespoon olive oil
Juice of ½ lemon
Salt and pepper to taste
½ teaspoon chili flakes
1 clove garlic, minced

Directions
1. Place the chicken drumsticks in a large bowl.
2. Season with salt and pepper to taste and the soy sauce, olive oil, lemon juice, chili flakes, and minced garlic.
3. Mix until combined and coat the drumsticks with the mixture.
4. Place the drumsticks in a baking tray lined with parchment paper and bake in a preheated oven at 350°F (180°C) for 20–25 minutes.
5. Served with steamed broccoli or green beans, if desired.

Nutrition (per serving)
Calories 297, fat 19.4 g, carbs 5.2 g, sugar 3.9 g
Protein 25.6 g, sodium 595 mg

Creamy Tuscan Chicken

Chicken is always good when there is a creamy sauce in the skillet that goes well with it. Be sure to have some crusty bread on hand, because the sauce is everything you could wish for! Once you try it, you are going to make it every week for lunch or dinner.

Prep time 10 minutes | Cooking time 25 minutes

Ingredients
1 boneless skinless chicken breast
Salt and pepper to taste
2 teaspoons olive oil
½ teaspoon dried oregano
1 clove garlic, minced
1 cup baby spinach
1 tablespoon grated Parmesan cheese
Juice of 1 lemon
¼ cup heavy cream

Directions
1. Warm the olive oil in a medium skillet over medium heat.
2. Add the chicken breast and season with salt and pepper to taste and the oregano.
3. Cook until golden brown and no longer pink. Remove from the skillet and set aside.
4. To the same skillet, add the heavy cream baby spinach, lemon juice, and garlic. Return the chicken.
5. Cook for 5 minutes, until the spinach, is translucent.
6. Serve the chicken with the sauce on top.

Nutrition (per serving)
Calories 425, fat 30 g, carbs 6.6 g, sugar 2.3 g
Protein 32.8 g, sodium 367 mg

Turkey Meatballs

To make this simple recipe, you will need just a few simple ingredients. To make them super healthy, you just need to bake them instead of frying them in a frying pan. To make everything healthier, my recipe uses ground rolled oats instead of breadcrumbs, and they are scrumptious.

Prep time 10 minutes | Cooking time 20 minutes

Ingredients
½ pound ground turkey
¼ cup ground rolled oats
¼ cup chopped onion
1 egg yolk
2 tablespoons chopped parsley
1 clove garlic, minced
Salt and pepper to taste
½ teaspoon dried basil
½ teaspoon dried oregano
2 tablespoons olive oil

Directions
1. Place the turkey, oats, onion, egg yolk, parsley, garlic, salt and pepper to taste, basil, and oregano in a large mixing bowl and mix until combined.
2. Oil your hands with olive oil and form small meatballs from the turkey mixture.
3. Arrange the meatballs on a baking tray lined with parchment paper and bake in a preheated oven at 350°F (180°C) for 20–25 minutes.
4. Serve warm with a baby spinach salad on the side.

Nutrition (per serving)
Calories 799, fat 58.5 g, carbs 12.3 g, sugar 1.6 g
Protein 67.1 g, sodium 259 mg

Turkey and Sweet Potato Casserole

This is one of those meals that are super delicious and ready in less than 30 minutes. You are going to be amazed at how flavorful it is. This is a one-pan recipe that you are going to love making for yourself.

Prep time 10 minutes | Cooking time 25 minutes

Ingredients
1 tablespoon olive oil
½ pound ground turkey
Salt and pepper to taste
½ teaspoon garlic powder
¼ cup onion, diced
¾ cup sweet potato, diced
½ teaspoon chili powder
¼ cup shredded mozzarella cheese
1 tablespoon chopped parsley

Directions
1. Warm the olive oil in a medium skillet over medium heat.
2. Add the garlic powder and diced onion. Cook for 5 minutes.
3. Stir in the ground turkey and cook for 5 minutes until the meat is no longer pink.
4. Stir in the diced sweet potato and season with the chili powder and salt and pepper to taste. Cover and cook 10 minutes more.
5. Top with the shredded mozzarella and place the skillet in a preheated oven at 350°F (180°C) for about 10 minutes more.
6. Sprinkle freshly chopped parsley on top and serve.

Nutrition (per serving)
Calories 740, fat 40.7 g, carbs 36 g, sugar 11.4 g
Protein 67.9 g, sodium 356 mg

Duck Breast with Orange Sauce

Cooking duck breast can be a little bit tricky. It's very important to not dry out the meat while cooking it, but with my recipe, I am sure you will have juicy and fragrant duck breast. The secret is in the orange sauce.

Prep time 10 minutes | Cooking time 20 minutes

Ingredients
1 duck breast
1 tablespoon butter
1 clove garlic, minced
1 teaspoon lemon peel
2 tablespoons breadcrumbs
½ teaspoon dried oregano

Orange Marinade
¼ cup orange juice
2 teaspoons balsamic vinegar
1 tablespoon olive oil
1 tablespoon honey
¼ cup lemon juice
Salt and pepper to taste

Directions
1. Place the orange juice, balsamic vinegar, olive oil, honey, lemon juice, and salt and pepper to taste in a large mixing bowl.
2. Add the minced clove garlic, lemon peel, and oregano.
3. Place the duck breast in the marinade and let it steep for 5 minutes.
4. Remove the duck breast from the marinade, coat it with breadcrumbs, and place it in a baking tray lined with parchment paper spread with butter.

5. Bake the duck breast for about 25 minutes in a preheated oven at 350°F (180°C).
6. While the duck breast is roasting, place the orange marinade in a saucepan over medium heat and bring to a boil. Cook for 15 minutes.
7. Slice the duck breast and drizzle it with warm orange marinade before serving.

Nutrition (per serving)
Calories 598, fat 33.4 g, carbs 36.8 g, sugar 24.8 g
Protein 38.4 g, sodium 195 mg

BEEF, PORK, LAMB, AND VEAL

Pineapple Pork Stir Fry

This is an exotic recipe that will make one healthy bowl of warming dinner or lunch. It's delicious, fragrant, and will require almost no time to prepare.

Prep time 10 minutes | Cooking time 25 minutes

Ingredients
½ pound pork chops
2 teaspoons olive oil
Salt and pepper to taste
2 tablespoons soy sauce
2 tablespoons rice vinegar
1 tablespoon honey
1 clove garlic, minced
½ teaspoon grated ginger
¼ pineapple, peeled and diced
1 spring onion, diced

Directions
1. Warm the olive oil in a large frying pan. Add the diced onion.
2. Place the pork chops in the warm oil and cook for about 5 minutes on each side.
3. Stir in the pineapple, ginger, garlic, honey, soy sauce, and rice vinegar and season with salt and pepper to taste.
4. Cook for about 10 minutes more.
5. Serve warm.

Nutrition (per serving)
Calories 940, fat 65.9 g, carbs 27.9 g, sugar 22.3 g
Protein 53.8 g, sodium 1967 mg

Crisp Parmesan Pork Loin Steak

Not only is this delicious and easy to make, but prepared this way (roasted), it makes a perfect healthy lunch idea that will feed you while you are living your busy life. To make it presentable just for yourself, serve it with a mixed green salad with a simple vinaigrette dressing that has olive oil, Dijon mustard, and salt and pepper to taste.

Prep time 10 minutes | Cooking time 25 minutes

Ingredients
½ pound pork loin steaks
Salt and pepper to taste
1 tablespoon olive oil
1 egg, lightly beaten
1 tablespoon buttermilk
1 tablespoon grated Parmesan cheese
1 tablespoon breadcrumbs
½ teaspoon dried rosemary

Directions
1. Season the pork loin steaks with salt and pepper to taste.
2. Coat the pork loin steaks with the lightly beaten egg and the buttermilk.
3. In another bowl, whisk together the Parmesan cheese, rosemary, and breadcrumbs.
4. Coat the pork loin steaks with the breadcrumbs and place them in a baking tray lined with parchment paper.
5. Drizzle with olive oil and bake in a preheated oven at 350°F (180°C) for 20–25 minutes.
6. Serve with a mixed green salad.

Nutrition (per serving)
Calories 698, fat 49.2 g, carbs 9.4 g, sugar 3.5 g
Protein 59.1 g, sodium 1725 mg

BBQ Meatballs

These barbecue meatballs are tasty and tangy because of the easy homemade barbecue sauce. This meal is delicious and healthy because there's no added sugar in the sauce. You can always bake the meatballs instead of frying, but the recipe itself is healthy and delicious as it is.

Prep time 10 minutes | Cooking time 25 minutes

Ingredients
½ pound ground beef
2 teaspoons olive oil
2 tablespoons finely diced onion
1 clove garlic, minced
2 tablespoons chopped parsley
1 egg yolk
½ teaspoon chili powder
Salt and pepper to taste
½ teaspoon chili flakes
BBQ Sauce:
½ cup ketchup
1 teaspoon apple cider vinegar
½ teaspoon garlic powder
1 teaspoon chili powder
1 teaspoon ground mustard
Salt and pepper to taste
1 tablespoon honey

Directions
1. In a large bowl, mix the ketchup, apple cider vinegar, garlic powder, chili powder, ground mustard, salt and pepper to taste, and honey.
2. In another bowl, mix the ground beef, diced onion, garlic, parsley, egg yolk, chili powder, salt, and

pepper to taste and chili flakes. Form small meatballs.
3. Warm the olive oil in a nonstick frying pan over medium heat and cook the meatballs on each side for about 5 minutes.
4. Pour in the homemade BBQ sauce and cook for about 5 minutes more.
5. Serve in a bowl.

Nutrition (per serving)
Calories 776, fat 29.6 g, carbs 54.5 g, sugar 46.3 g
Protein 75.5 g, sodium 1515 mg

Veal Chops with Salsa

Veal chops make a healthy supper while you are living your busy life. You are going to enjoy it even more with refreshing green salsa on the side to enhance the flavor. The lemon gives a refreshing taste in the marinade as well as in the salsa, and instead of frying, you can bake the veal chop wrapped in the foil for more tender meat.

Prep time 10 minutes | Cooking time 25 minutes

Ingredients
1 British rose veal chop
½ teaspoon paprika
2 teaspoons breadcrumbs
2 cloves garlic, minced
Zest of ½ lemon
¼ cup olive oil
Salsa:
½ green pepper, finely diced
1 clove garlic, minced
2 tablespoons olive oil
Zest of ½ lemon
1 cup baby spinach
1 green chili, finely diced

Directions
1. Sprinkle the veal chop with the paprika, breadcrumbs, minced garlic, and lemon zest.
2. Warm the olive oil in a nonstick frying pan over medium heat and cook the veal chop for 7–8 minutes on each side.
3. Place the green pepper, garlic, olive oil, lemon zest, baby spinach, and green chili in a food processor and blitz until a fine salsa develops.
4. Serve the salsa on top of the veal chop.

Nutrition (per serving)
Calories 1432, fat 51 g, carbs 14.1 g, sugar 2.1 g
Protein 2.5 g, sodium 2764 mg

Veal Piccata

This recipe requires the veal to be cut into very thin slices—that's essential for this recipe. The creamy sauce is delicious and gives a nice shiny look to the veal cutlets. The capers and wine give a rich taste and a tender texture to the meat itself.

Prep time 10 minutes | Cooking time 20 minutes

Ingredients
3 ounces veal top round cutlets
Salt and pepper to taste
2 tablespoons butter
1 tablespoon olive oil
¼ cup white wine
¾ cup chicken stock
¼ cup all-purpose flour
1 lemon, cut into circles
2 tablespoons capers
2 tablespoons freshly chopped parsley

Directions
1. Melt the butter and warm the olive oil in a nonstick frying pan on medium heat.
2. Cook the veal cutlets for 3–4 minutes on each side.
3. Season with salt and pepper to taste.
4. Sprinkle with the flour and cook for 1 minute.
5. Stir in the wine and chicken stock together and cook until a creamy sauce develops.
6. Stir in the lemon circles, capers, and freshly chopped parsley.
7. Cook for 10 minutes on medium heat.
8. Serve the veal cutlets with the creamy sauce on top.

Nutrition (per serving)
Calories 608, fat 40.4 g, carbs 32.8 g, sugar 2.7 g
Protein 22.6 g, sodium 1323 mg

Greek-Style Lamb with Green Beans

Lamb is one of the healthiest meats and prepared this way, it will fill you up with Proteins, nutrients, and vitamins that are essential for a healthy lifestyle. Even if it's cooked for one, cook up a storm and enjoy the meal.

Prep time 10 minutes | Cooking time 20 minutes

½ pound lamb steak
Zest and juice of ½ lemon
1 clove garlic, minced
1 tablespoon olive oil
½ pound green beans
Salt and pepper to taste
2 ounces feta cheese, crumbled

Directions
1. Season the lamb steak with the lemon zest and juice.
2. Rub the minced garlic, olive oil, and salt and pepper to taste into the lamb steak.
3. Warm the olive oil in a nonstick frying pan over medium heat and add the lamb steak.
4. Cook for about 8 minutes on each side.
5. Bring salted water to a simmer in a saucepan. Add the green beans and cook for 4–6 minutes until tender.
6. Serve the green beans with the lamb. Sprinkle the crumbled feta cheese on top and season with ground black pepper to taste.

Nutrition (per serving)
Calories 783, fat 43.2 g, carbs 25 g, sugar 7 g
Protein 76.7 g, sodium 820 mg

Beef and Broccoli

Beef couldn't be healthier and tastier than this recipe. Prepared with broccoli, you are not going to believe how tasty it is. This is ready in almost no time, so prepare for your next dinner and enjoy.

Prep time 10 minutes | Cooking time 25 minutes

Ingredients
½ pound lean beefsteak
1 tablespoon cornstarch
½ pound broccoli florets
¼ cup soy sauce
1 clove garlic, minced
Salt and pepper to taste
2 tablespoons water
1 tablespoon olive oil

Directions
Warm the olive oil in a medium skillet on medium heat. Cut the steak into small strips and season with salt and pepper to taste. Coat with cornstarch.
Add to the warm oil.
Stir in the broccoli florets, soy sauce, garlic, and water. Cook until a creamy sauce forms in the pan.

Nutrition (per serving)
Calories 688, fat 28.9 g, carbs 28.3 g, sugar 5 g
Protein 79.4 g, sodium 3820 mg

Lamb Stuffed Zucchinis

Prep time 10 minutes | Cooking time 25 minutes

1 medium zucchini
Salt and pepper to taste
½ pound ground lamb
1 tablespoon olive oil
1 teaspoon paprika powder
1 clove garlic, minced
½ teaspoon dried oregano

Directions
1. Cut the zucchini in half lengthwise and scoop out the middle part.
2. Mix the ground lamb, salt, and pepper to taste, paprika powder, garlic, and oregano in a bowl.
3. Fill the middle part of the zucchini with the ground meat mixture and bake in a preheated oven at 350°F (180°C) for 20–25 minutes.
4. Serve warm.

Nutrition (per serving)
Calories 806, fat 59.3 g, carbs 9.3 g, sugar 3.7 g
Protein 59.1 g, sodium 205 mg

FISH AND SEAFOOD

Garlic Shrimp with Quinoa

Are you looking for an easy, quick, and delicious supper meal that will warm you up on a cold winter day? Fresh lemon and garlic are the secret ingredients that make this meal so special. You can adjust the spiciness by adding more or fewer chili flakes.

Prep time 10 minutes | Cooking time 30 minutes

Ingredients
1 tablespoon olive oil
½ pound shrimp
Salt and pepper to taste
½ teaspoon chili flakes
2 tablespoons finely diced onion
2 cloves garlic, minced
½ cup quinoa
¼ teaspoon paprika
1 cup chicken broth
2 tablespoons finely chopped parsley

Directions
1. Warm the olive oil in a nonstick frying pan over medium heat.
2. Add the diced onion and cook for 5 minutes.
3. Stir in the cleaned shrimp and cook for 3–4 minutes.
4. Season with salt and pepper to taste and the chili flakes, garlic, paprika, and quinoa.
5. Pour in the chicken broth and cook for another 20 minutes on low until the quinoa is cooked through.

6. Serve the quinoa and shrimp with freshly chopped parsley.

Nutrition (per serving)
Calories 763, fat 24.5 g, carbs 63.6 g, sugar 1.8 g
Protein 69.4 g, sodium 1328 mg

Orange Salmon with Spinach Salad

Salmon is one of the most delicious dishes in the world. Baked on top of orange circles it has a nice and flavorful taste that will tickle your taste buds. You will only need 20 minutes to bake the salmon, and while that's in the oven, you can make a baby spinach salad with a simple but tasty vinaigrette.

Prep time 5 minutes | Cooking time 20 minutes

Ingredients
1 tablespoon olive oil
½ orange, sliced in circles
1 (8-ounce) salmon fillet
Salt and pepper to taste
1 teaspoon dried oregano
Salad:
2 cups baby spinach
Salt and pepper to taste
1 tablespoon olive oil
1 teaspoon Dijon mustard
½ teaspoon dried oregano

Directions
1. Arrange the orange slices on a baking dish lined with parchment paper and place the salmon fillet on top.
2. Season with salt and pepper to taste, sprinkle on the oregano, and drizzle with the olive oil.
3. Bake in a preheated oven at 350°F (180°C) for 15–20 minutes.
4. While the fish is cooking, place the baby spinach in a bowl. In another bowl, mix the olive oil, Dijon mustard, salt and pepper, and oregano together.
5. Drizzle the vinaigrette onto the baby spinach.
6. Serve the fish with the baby spinach salad.

Nutrition (per serving)
Calories 605, fat 42.7 g, carbs 14.3 g, sugar 9 g
Protein 47 g, sodium 204 mg

Healthy Baked Salmon

If you prepare your salmon this way, you will end up with flaky, tender fish that is ready in just 30 minutes. This makes a perfect dinner or lunch, and the amount of Protein in the fish is all you need to keep your lifestyle healthy.

Prep time 5 minutes | Cooking time 20 minutes

Ingredients
6 ounces salmon fillet
1 tablespoon olive oil
Salt and pepper to taste
1 clove garlic, minced
½ teaspoon Italian seasoning
Juice of ½ lemon

Directions
1. Grease a baking dish with olive oil and place the salmon fillet on top.
2. Season with salt and pepper to taste.
3. In a small bowl, whisk together the olive oil, minced garlic, Italian seasoning, and lemon juice.
4. Spoon the seasonings over the salmon and rub them into the fish.
5. Bake in a preheated oven at 400°F (190°C) for 15–18 minutes.
6. Cover with aluminum foil and let cool for 5 minutes.
7. Serve warm.

Nutrition (per serving)
Calories 370, fat 25.4 g, carbs 5.5 g, sugar 6 g
Protein 33.4 g, sodium 77 mg

Honey and Garlic Shrimp

The sweetness from the honey and the earthy taste from the garlic makes this recipe so special. Serve it with simple steamed broccoli and you will have a plate full of nutrients for a perfect healthy lifestyle. Make it spicy with an additional sprinkle of chili flakes, or leave without if you don't like spicy food.

Prep time 5 minutes | Cooking time 20 minutes

Ingredients
2 tablespoons honey
2 tablespoons soy sauce
2 cloves garlic, minced
½ pound shrimp, cleaned
2 teaspoons olive oil
Salt and pepper to taste
2 cups broccoli florets

Directions
1. Warm the olive oil in a large nonstick frying pan over medium heat.
2. Cook the shrimp for 2–3 minutes on each side.
3. Season with minced garlic and salt and pepper to taste. Add the soy sauce and honey.
4. Cook for 7–8 minutes and then set aside to cool.
5. Steam the broccoli florets over boiling water.
6. Serve the steamed broccoli florets and honey-garlic shrimp in a bowl with cooked rice.

Nutrition (per serving)
Calories 565, fat 13.8 g, carbs 54.6 g, sugar 38.2 g
Protein 59.3 g, sodium 2420 mg

Shrimp Zoodles

Okay, this is a much healthier version of pasta alfredo. And even though this is a gluten-free version of the famous pasta and shrimp dish, you will be amazed at how delicious this recipe is. Creamy and flavorful, you are going to forget about the classic pasta recipes and make this zoodle shrimp supper from now on.

Prep time 10 minutes | Cooking time 20 minutes

Ingredients
1 tablespoon olive oil
1 small onion, diced
1 clove garlic, minced
½ pound shrimp, cleaned
Salt and pepper to taste
½ teaspoon chili flakes
Zest of ½ lemon
½ pound zucchini noodles (zoodles)
2 tablespoons chopped parsley
2 tablespoons grated Parmesan cheese

Directions
1. Warm the olive oil in a large nonstick frying pan over medium heat and cook the diced onion for 2–3 minutes until tender.
2. Stir in the minced garlic and shrimp.
3. Season with salt and pepper to taste and the chili flakes, lemon zest, and zoodles.
4. Cook for 10 minutes until the shrimp are cooked and pink in color.
5. Stir in the freshly chopped parsley and Parmesan cheese and serve warm.

Nutrition (per serving)
Calories 552, fat 24.4 g, carbs 20.5 g, sugar 7.1 g
Protein 64.6 g, sodium 844 mg

Garlic Herbed Frilled Tuna Steak

If you have access to tuna steak, you can make a 5-star restaurant tuna steak that will be well worth trying. It's easy, it's quick, and it's delicious. The most important thing while cooking tuna is not to overcook it.

Prep time 5 minutes | Cooking time 20 minutes

Ingredients
1 tablespoon lemon juice
1 tablespoon olive oil
1 clove garlic, minced
½ teaspoon dried thyme
6 ounces of tuna steak
Salt and pepper to taste

Directions
1. Place the tuna steak in a large bowl and season with salt and pepper to taste.
2. Drizzle with lemon juice, olive oil, and minced garlic. Sprinkle the dried thyme on top and let it steep for 5–10 minutes.
3. Warm a nonstick frying pan over medium heat and place the tuna steak in the hot pan.
4. Cook for 2–3 minutes, flip, and cook for the same time on the other side.
5. Serve with a mixed green salad.

Nutrition (per serving)
Calories 443, fat 24.9 g, carbs 1.7 g, sugar 0.4 g
Protein 51.3 g, sodium 89 mg

VEGETARIAN

Caponata Pasta

Are you living a busy life? If your answer is yes, then you are going to love this pasta recipe that is ready in under 20 minutes, loaded with tomato sauce, basil, and Parmesan cheese. It's never too late to have a nice pasta bowl that is filling and delicious.

Prep time 5 minutes | Cooking time 20 minutes

Ingredients
1 tablespoon olive oil
¼ cup onion, chopped
1 clove garlic, minced
½ small eggplant, diced
1 red bell pepper, diced
1½ cups tomato sauce
1½ cups rigatoni
2 tablespoons basil, chopped
2 tablespoons grated Parmesan

Directions
1. Warm the olive oil in a large saucepan over medium heat and add the diced onion and minced garlic.
2. Stir in the diced eggplant and red bell pepper and cook for 10 minutes.
3. Stir in the tomato sauce and rigatoni.
4. Cook for 10 minutes until the pasta is tender and cooked through.
5. Stir in a bowl topped with the freshly chopped basil and grated Parmesan.

Nutrition (per serving)
Calories 876, fat 23.7 g, carbs 141.6 g, sugar 34.3 g
Protein 34.5 g, sodium 2201 mg

Gnocchi with Mushrooms and Blue Cheese

If you are running out of time, you can use store-bought gnocchi for this recipe, but if you want you can also make them from scratch. Gnocchi is made from mashed potatoes, flour, eggs, and salt. The recipe is simple, but it does take some time. Nevertheless, you are going to love the combination of gnocchi, blue cheese, and mushrooms. It's perfect as a supper to feed your hungry soul after a busy, hardworking day.

Prep time 5 minutes | Cooking time 25 minutes

Ingredients
7 ounces fresh gnocchi
1 tablespoon olive oil
Salt and pepper to taste
1 spring onion, diced
5 ounces fresh mushrooms, diced
1 clove garlic, minced
3 ounces creamy blue cheese
1 tablespoon freshly chopped parsley

Directions
1. Cook the fresh gnocchi in a large pot with boiling salted water until they rise to the surface.
2. Remove from the water and set aside.
3. In a medium frying pan over medium heat, warm the olive oil and cook the diced spring onion and diced mushrooms.
4. Stir in the minced garlic and season with salt and pepper to taste.
5. Stir in the cooked gnocchi and cook for 5–10 minutes.

6. Stir in the blue cheese and mix until creamy and combined.
7. Serve in a bowl with freshly chopped parsley.

Nutrition (per serving)
Calories 756, fat 39.2 g, carbs 78.9 g, sugar 2.8 g
Protein 31.2 g, sodium 955 mg

Sweetcorn and Zucchini Fritters

In around 30 minutes you can have the healthiest fritters on the table. Instead of frying them, you will bake them for a much healthier version. They are good for dinner or lunch, and you can combine them with your favorite salad.

Prep time 5 minutes | Cooking time 25 minutes

Ingredients
1 tablespoon olive oil
½ cup sweetcorn
1 small zucchini, grated
1 spring onion, finely diced
1 large egg
2 tablespoons all-purpose flour
½ teaspoon chili flakes
½ teaspoon baking powder
Salt and pepper to taste

Directions
1. Place the sweetcorn, grated zucchini, diced spring onion, egg, chili flakes, baking powder, and flour in a large mixing bowl. Season with salt and pepper to taste and mix until combined.
2. Use an ice cream scoop to place the zucchini fritters in a baking pan lined with parchment paper.
3. Drizzle a little oil on top of the fritters and flatten them with a spatula.
4. Bake in a preheated oven at 350°F (180°C) for 20–25 minutes until golden brown and cooked through.
5. Serve with a mixed green salad.

Nutrition (per serving)
Calories 341, fat 20.3 g, carbs 33.2 g, sugar 5.4 g
Protein 12.1 g, sodium 98 mg

Easy Vegetarian Quesadilla

Customize your favorite veggie filling into this quesadilla. It's easy, it's fast, and it's tasty. Quesadillas are always a great option if you are running out of recipe ideas and want to cook up something very quick and delicious.

Prep time 10 minutes | Cooking time 10 minutes

Ingredients
1 tablespoon olive oil
2 flour tortillas
½ cup sweet corn
½ cup frozen peas
½ cup black beans
1 small jalapeño, finely diced
1 cup grated mozzarella cheese
Salt and pepper to taste

Directions
1. Brush a tortilla with olive oil and fill it with sweet corn, frozen peas, black beans, and diced jalapeño.
2. Season with salt and pepper to taste and sprinkle with mozzarella.
3. Cover with the other tortilla and place the quesadilla brushed side down on a nonstick frying pan over medium heat.
4. Cook for 2–3 minutes on each side.
5. Cut into 6 triangles and serve warm.

Nutrition (per serving)
Calories 768, fat 23 g, carbs 109.7 g, sugar 9.2 g
Protein 38.5 g, sodium 266 mg

Mushroom Bhaji

This Indian inspired recipe is basically mushroom stir fry. It's seasoned perfectly with a variety of seasonings and it's ready in under 20 minutes. That's all you need for a perfect lunch or dinner.

Prep time 5 minutes | Cooking time 10 minutes

Ingredients
1 tablespoon olive oil
½ pound fresh chestnut mushrooms
½ small onion, diced
1 clove garlic, minced
½ teaspoon ground cumin
½ teaspoon ground coriander
½ teaspoon ground turmeric
1 tablespoon tomato paste
1 cup cooked rice for serving

Directions
1. Warm the olive oil in a nonstick frying pan over medium heat and add the diced mushrooms and onion.
2. Stir in the garlic.
3. Season with cumin, coriander, turmeric, and tomato paste.
4. Cook for about 5 minutes.
5. Boil the rice in two parts water and a little bit of salt in a saucepan over medium heat.
6. Serve the mushrooms in a bowl with the cooked rice.

Nutrition (per serving)
Calories 883, fat 16.4 g, carbs 163.8 g, sugar 7.6 g
Protein 21.9 g, sodium 42 mg

Coconut and Squash Curry

If you want to make something easy and fragrant, this coconut and squash curry is ready in under 20 minutes. This is a heartwarming meal that will keep you full on a busy winter day, not to mention that it has the most delicious veggie—pumpkin.

Prep time 5 minutes | Cooking time 15 minutes

Ingredients
1½ cups butternut squash, peeled and diced
1 tablespoon olive oil
1 small onion, diced
1 tablespoon curry paste
Salt and pepper to taste
½ cup chopped tomatoes
¾ cup coconut milk
½ cup red lentils
1 cup baby spinach
2 tablespoons yogurt, for serving

Directions
1. Warm the olive oil in a medium saucepan over medium heat.
2. Add the diced onion and squash.
3. Stir in the curry paste, tomatoes, red lentils, and coconut oil. Season with salt and pepper to taste.
4. Cook for 10–15 minutes until the squash is tender.
5. Stir in the baby spinach and cook for 1 minute more.
6. Serve in a bowl with yogurt.

Nutrition (per serving)
Calories 1056, fat 58.9 g, carbs 108.6 g, sugar 21.2 g
Protein 35.2 g, sodium 484 mg

Veggie Fajita

If you are a big fan of Mexican food, then you are going to love this veggie fajita. This meat-free fajita is loaded with black beans, avocado, and peppers. It will take you only 15 minutes to make it.

Prep time 5 minutes | Cooking time 15 minutes

Ingredients
½ cup black beans, drained
1 large flour tortilla
½ avocado, sliced
1 tablespoon sour cream
Fajita Mix:
1 red pepper, cut into strips
1 yellow pepper, cut into strips
1 tablespoon olive oil
1 clove garlic, minced
½ teaspoon chili powder
½ teaspoon chili flakes
½ teaspoon ground cumin
½ small onion, cut into wedges
Salt and pepper to taste

Directions
1. Warm the olive oil in a nonstick frying pan over medium heat and add the diced red and yellow pepper, minced garlic, and onion.
2. Mix until combined and season with salt and pepper to taste, chili powder, chili flakes, and ground cumin.
3. Cook for 7–10 minutes until the peppers and onions are translucent.
4. Spread the sour cream on the tortilla and add the black beans and avocado slices.

5. Arrange the cooked fajita mix on top of the tortilla and wrap it tightly.

Nutrition (per serving)
Calories 849, fat 39.4 g, carbs 16.7 g, sugar 10.4 g
Protein 28.6 g, sodium 52 mg

Spinach and Ricotta Stuffed Shells

This recipe is for one of those days when you want to create something delicious and when you are not in a hurry. The shells are first boiled for 2–3 minutes so they can be easily stuffed with the most delicious ricotta and spinach filling. The best part comes when they are touched by tomato sauce and melty mozzarella cheese while baked in the oven.

Prep time 5 minutes | Cooking time 25 minutes

Ingredients
½ pound pasta shells
1 tablespoon olive oil
2 cups spinach
4 ounces ricotta cheese
Salt and pepper to taste
1½ cups tomato sauce
3 ounces shredded mozzarella cheese
½ teaspoon dried oregano

Directions
1. Bring a pot of salted water to a boil and cook the pasta shells for 2–3 minutes.
2. Drain the pasta shells and arrange them in a baking pan drizzled with olive oil.
3. In another bowl, mix the ricotta cheese with the spinach and season it with salt and pepper to taste.
4. Stuff the pasta shells with the spinach and ricotta filling and arrange them back in the baking pan.
5. Pour the tomato sauce over the stuffed pasta shells and sprinkle the grated mozzarella cheese and dried oregano on top.
6. Bake the stuffed pasta shells in a preheated oven at 350°F (180°C) for 20–25 minutes.

7. Serve warm.

Nutrition (per serving)
Calories 1274, fat 44.2 g, carbs 155.5 g, sugar 16.3 g
Protein 69.2 g, sodium 2684 mg

SNACKS AND SMALL BITES

Smoked Salmon Cucumber Bites

These smoked salmon cucumber bites are a big hit at anyone's party, but why don't you make them for a snack on a busy day? They are easy to put together and you will love the refreshing taste of the cucumber and Greek yogurt filling. To bring all the flavors together, there's smoked salmon too.

Prep time 10 minutes

Ingredients
½ English cucumber, peeled and sliced in ½-inch circles
½ cup Greek yogurt
½ teaspoon dried oregano
½ teaspoon dried dill
¼ teaspoon garlic powder
Salt and pepper to taste
2 ounces smoked salmon

Directions
1. Arrange the cucumber circles on a plate.
2. In a small bowl, mix the Greek yogurt, oregano, dill, and garlic powder and season with salt and pepper to taste.
3. Fill the cucumber circles with the yogurt mixture and top them with smoked salmon.
4. Serve right away.

Nutrition (per serving)
Calories 171, fat 4.8 g, carbs 10.8 g, sugar 6.7g
Protein 21.7 g, sodium 1171 mg

Greek Salad with Goat Cheese

Greek salad is one of the most famous salads in the world, but traditionally Greek salad is made with feta cheese. I am making a little twist and make it lighter by using goat cheese.

Prep time 10 minutes

Ingredients
1 ripe tomato, cut into ½-inch pieces
½ small cucumber, peeled and diced
1 small red onion, sliced in half-moons
4 Kalamata olives, pitted and diced
1 tablespoon freshly chopped mint
2 ounces goat cheese, diced
2 teaspoons olive oil
Salt and pepper to taste

Directions
1. Place the tomato pieces in a medium bowl and stir in the diced cucumber and red onion half-moons.
2. Top with the Kalamata olives, mint, and goat cheese.
3. Drizzle with olive oil and season with salt and pepper to taste.
4. Mix and serve immediately.

Nutrition (per serving)
Calories 421, fat 31.8 g, carbs 17.3 g, sugar 8.3 g
Protein 20 g, sodium 360 mg

Fresh Cherry Tomato Bruschetta

Life is so much tastier with bruschetta. I am always wondering how these little pieces of crunchy bread topped with spread (or cheese) and fresh cherry tomatoes make me (and so many others) so happy! The best part is the final drizzle of olive oil and freshly chopped basil that gives the best taste to this snack.

Prep time 10 minutes | Cooking time 5 minutes

Ingredients
2 pieces ciabatta bread
2 teaspoons olive oil
Salt and pepper to taste
1 clove garlic, whole
2 tablespoons herbed cream cheese
6 cherry tomatoes, halved
1 tablespoon chopped basil

Directions
1. Toast the ciabatta bread and rub the garlic on the warm piece of bread.
2. Spread the cream cheese on the warm bread and season with salt and pepper to taste.
3. Top with the halved cherry tomatoes and sprinkle with freshly chopped basil.
4. Drizzle with a little tiny bit of olive oil and serve right away.

Nutrition (per serving)
Calories 1197, fat 52.1 g, carbs 153.6 g, sugar 41.4 g
Protein 36.6 g, sodium 1075 mg

Peanut Butter Apple Slices

This is so easy and ready in less than 5 minutes, but it's so filling and healthy! You can make it at your workplace, in your home, or while you are traveling around. All you have to do is spread some smooth or chunky peanut butter on a thick slice of apple and top it with raisins (or dried cranberries) and some chopped walnuts, almonds, or hazelnuts for a little crunch.

Prep time 5 minutes

Ingredients
1 apple, cut into 4 thick slices
2 tablespoons peanut butter
2 tablespoons raisins
2 tablespoons chopped walnuts
Honey (optional)

Directions
1. Arrange the apple slices and spread them with peanut butter.
2. Top with raisins and chopped walnuts. If you want a little sweet touch, drizzle a tiny bit of honey on each slice.
3. Serve right away.

Nutrition (per serving)
Calories 455, fat 25.8 g, carbs 53 g, sugar 37.1 g
Protein 12.9 g, sodium 151 mg

Dark Chocolate Bark with Almonds

The chocolate itself can be a good snack, but what about dark chocolate enriched with chopped almonds, coconut flakes, and cranberries? This can be ready in 5 minutes and enjoy for the whole day. You can even make a bigger batch for yourself and enjoy it throughout your busy week.

Prep time 10 minutes | Cooking time 10 minutes

Ingredients
3 ounces dark chocolate
3 tablespoons chopped almonds
1½ tablespoons coconut flakes
2 tablespoons dried cranberries
Pinch of sea salt flakes

Directions
1. Melt the chocolate and spread it over a baking paper with a spatula.
2. Before it solidifies, top it with the chopped almonds, coconut flakes, and cranberries.
3. Sprinkle on a pinch of sea salt flakes and let it sit for 2 minutes in the freezer.
4. Crack the chocolate bark to make smaller pieces before serving.

Nutrition (per serving)
Calories 592, fat 36.7 g, carbs 56.7 g, sugar 45.5 g
Protein 10.5 g, sodium 163 mg

Zucchini Baked Fries with Feta Cheese

When you first bite into these zucchini baked fries you are going to be amazed by their crunch. When all of that is topped with crumbled feta cheese, you end up with a delicious treat that you'll want to enjoy as a late-night snack.

Prep time 10 minutes | Cooking time 20 minutes

Ingredients
1 small zucchini, cut into 2-inch strips
1 medium egg, lightly beaten
Salt and pepper to taste
2 tablespoons all-purpose flour
3 tablespoons breadcrumbs
½ teaspoon dried oregano
¼ teaspoon garlic powder
½ teaspoon dried paprika

Directions
1. Arrange the zucchini pieces on a plate and cover them with flour.
2. In another bowl, mix the breadcrumbs with salt and pepper to taste and the oregano, garlic powder, and paprika.
3. Dip the zucchini pieces in the lightly beaten egg and cover them in the breadcrumb mixture.
4. Arrange them on a baking tray lined with parchment paper.
5. Bake in a preheated oven at 350°F (180°C) for 15–20 minutes until crispy and golden brown.

Nutrition (per serving)
Calories 227, fat 6 g, carbs 32.4 g, sugar 4 g
Protein 11.6 g, sodium 223 mg

Cheese Balls

I just love how easy this recipe is to prepare. There are only a few ingredients that just need to be combined in a bowl and then seasoned. You can prepare a double batch of these cottage cheese balls and bring them along whenever you travel, or just eat them in front of the TV without any doubts that you are eating healthily. After all, a cottage cheese ball is way better than a bag of potato chips.

Prep time 10 minutes

Ingredients
5 ounces of cottage cheese
Salt and pepper to taste
3 tablespoons cream cheese
½ teaspoon dried oregano
½ teaspoon chili flakes
½ teaspoon dried basil
Chopped parsley, toasted sesame seeds, chili flakes for rolling (optional)

Directions
1. In a medium bowl, stir together the cottage cheese, salt, and pepper to taste, cream cheese, oregano, chili flakes, and basil.
2. Form small balls from the mixture.
3. You can roll them in chopped parsley, toasted sesame seeds, and/or chili flakes, but there's nothing bad about serving them "naked."

Nutrition (per serving)
Calories 235, fat 13.3 g, carbs 6.6 g, sugar 0.6 g
Protein 21.9 g, sodium 665 mg

Avocado Toast with Chia Seeds

If you are feeling a little bit hungry, the avocado toast will make you feel full. The cream cheese spread will help you stick the avocado slices on, and the chia seeds will bring so many nutrients to your snack.

Prep time 5 minutes

Ingredients
1 slice wholegrain bread
2 tablespoons cream cheese
Salt and pepper to taste
½ avocado, sliced
1 teaspoon chia seeds
1 teaspoon olive oil

Directions
1. Spread the cream cheese on top of the whole grain bread and top with the sliced avocado.
2. Sprinkle with chia seeds and salt and pepper to taste.
3. Drizzle with olive oil just before serving.

Nutrition (per serving)
Calories 453, fat 36.5 g, carbs 26.8 g, sugar 2.1 g
Protein 9.4 g, sodium 200 mg

Grilled Polenta

Polenta is one of the healthiest ingredients that can be consumed for breakfast or a snack. To prepare it, you cook it in water and then cut it into triangles after it's cooled completely. After grilling it, you can take it wherever you want.

Prep time 10 minutes | Cooking time 10 minutes

Ingredients
1 cup water
Pinch of salt
½ cup polenta
Pinch of ground black pepper
1 teaspoon butter
1 tablespoon grated Parmesan cheese
1 teaspoon olive oil

Directions
1. Bring the water to a boil in a saucepan and season with salt and pepper to taste.
2. Add the polenta and cook until thickened.
3. Stir in the butter and grated Parmesan cheese and mix until smooth.
4. Pour the polenta into a small baking dish and let it cool completely.
5. Cut in squares and then cut each square diagonally into triangles.
6. Warm the olive oil in a grill pan and cook each triangle for about 2 minutes on each side, until grill marks appear.

Nutrition (per serving)
Calories 396, fat 12.2 g, carbs 61.4 g, sugar 0.8 g
Protein 10.3 g, sodium 322 mg

Chia Pudding with Three Ingredients

This next snack recipe can be made at night for the next day, and you can bring it whenever you want to go. It's a three-ingredient chia pudding containing almond milk, chia seeds, and honey. It's simple, but it will keep you full for a long period of time in a healthy way!

Prep time 5 minutes

Ingredients
½ cup almond milk
2 tablespoons chia seeds
1 tablespoon honey

Directions
1. Mix the almond milk, chia seeds, and honey together in a small jar.
2. Just to make sure it will set evenly, mix every 5 minutes for the first 15 minutes.
3. Let it steep in the fridge for 30 minutes to overnight.
4. To make it fancier, top with oats, fresh fruit, or chocolate chips.

Nutrition (per serving)
Calories 478, fat 37.3 g, carbs 35.9 g, sugar 21.3 g
Protein 7.5 g, sodium 23 mg

DESSERTS

Banana Pudding

There are hundreds of instant banana pudding packages in the supermarket, but I love making it from scratch, and this recipe is nothing less than simple, classic, silky smooth, and creamy. It's a decadent dessert that everyone will love, and with this recipe, you will learn how to make it for only yourself.

Prep time 5 minutes | Cooking time 5 minutes

Ingredients
½ cup whole milk
2 tablespoons sugar
2 teaspoons cornstarch
1 tablespoon butter
Pinch of salt
1 egg yolk
1 teaspoon vanilla extract
1 large banana, peeled and chopped
¼ cup graham cracker crumbs

Directions
1. Heat the milk in a medium saucepan over medium heat.
2. Stir in the sugar, cornstarch, salt, egg yolk, and vanilla.
3. When the mixture thickens, stir in the butter and set aside.
4. Stir the chopped banana into the warm pudding.
5. Place some graham cracker crumbs in a serving glass and top them with the banana pudding.

6. Top the pudding with more crushed graham crackers.
7. Chill and serve with crushed graham crackers or chopped banana.

Nutrition (per serving)
Calories 592, fat 23.3 g, carbs 88.4 g, sugar 56.5 g
Protein 10.2 g, sodium 468 mg

Mini Donuts

Donuts are always a great idea, but they are even greater if they are healthy, fast, and full of flavor. These are inspired by the flavors of autumn, and you are going to make the batter in just 5 minutes and wait another 5–7 minutes to bake them in a donut machine. If you do not have a mini doughnut machine, no worries—you will be able to bake them just as easily.

Prep time 5 minutes | Cooking time 5–7 minutes

Ingredients
⅓ cup almond milk
2 tablespoons honey
1 tablespoon olive oil
½ teaspoon vanilla extract
1 medium egg
½ cup almond flour
1 tablespoon coconut flakes
1 teaspoon baking powder
½ teaspoon ground cinnamon
¼ teaspoon ground nutmeg
Pinch of salt
2 tablespoons maple syrup

Directions
1. In a large mixing bowl, mix the almond milk, honey, olive oil, vanilla, and egg.
2. Stir in the almond flour, coconut flakes, baking powder, cinnamon, nutmeg, and salt.
3. Add tablespoonfuls of the donut batter to a preheated donut machine and cook, covered, for 5–7 minutes.
4. Alternatively, you can fry the donuts for 3–4 minutes until golden brown.

5. When done, coat with cinnamon sugar.
6. Serve with a drizzle of maple syrup.

Nutrition (per serving)
Calories 969, fat 66 g, carbs 82.8 g, sugar 62.1 g
Protein 19.8 g, sodium 260 mg

Peanut Butter Mug Cake

Peanut butter cake can be much healthier and prepared for a single serving. This recipe is a perfect treat for a busy day. When it comes to its taste, you will experience something between a peanut butter cookie and a fudgy piece of cake.

Prep time 5 minutes

Ingredients
1 tablespoon vegetable oil
2 tablespoons peanut butter
2 tablespoons sugar
1 egg yolk
2 tablespoons all-purpose flour
¼ teaspoon baking powder
2 tablespoons whole milk

Directions
1. Place the vegetable oil, peanut butter, sugar, and egg yolk in a microwave-safe mug.
2. Mix until combined and stir in the flour, baking powder, and milk.
3. Microwave the mug cake for 90 seconds on medium heat.
4. Serve with a little dollop of smooth peanut butter.

Nutrition (per serving)
Calories 528, fat 35.4 g, carbs 44.8 g, sugar 28.7 g
Protein 13.3 g, sodium 169 mg

Devil Chocolate Cake in a Mug

Making cakes for only one person is possible, and you can always make a double batch to satisfy your sweet tooth. This recipe contains dark cocoa powder to make it delicious and richly chocolaty in flavor. The vanilla extract gives an exotic touch and the honey makes it sweet in a much healthier way!

Prep time 5 minutes | Cooking time 5 minutes

Ingredients
2 tablespoons all-purpose flour
1 tablespoon honey
2 teaspoons dark cocoa powder
Pinch of salt
2 tablespoons whole milk
1 teaspoon olive oil
¼ teaspoon vanilla extract
Pinch of baking powder

Directions
1. Combine the flour, honey, cocoa powder, salt, milk, olive oil, and vanilla in a mug.
2. Mix until combined and stir in the pinch of baking powder.
3. Microwave for 1 minute on medium to high.
4. Serve with a drizzle of honey or a sprinkle of cocoa powder.

Nutrition (per serving)
Calories 202, fat 6.8 g, carbs 37 g, sugar 19 g
Protein 4.6 g, sodium 299 mg

No-Bake Cookie Balls

These are thick, chocolaty, and peanut buttery in flavor. They contain six simple but wholesome ingredients that are good for your body. This recipe makes a batch of four cookie balls, which is more than enough for a little treat on a busy day when you want something healthy and sweet at the same time.

Prep time 5 minutes

Ingredients
¼ cup peanut butter
1 tablespoon honey
2 tablespoons almond milk
⅔ cup quick-cooking oats
⅓ cup chocolate chips
½ teaspoon vanilla extract

Directions
1. Stir the butter together with the honey, almond milk, and vanilla in a medium mixing bowl.
2. Stir in the oats and chocolate chips and form a cookie dough.
3. Chill slightly in the fridge and then form 4–5 small balls.
4. You can dip them in dark chocolate or enjoy them as they are because they have chocolate chips inside.

Nutrition (per serving)
Calories 1024, fat 59.8 g, carbs 102.1 g, sugar 54 g
Protein 28.3 g, sodium 349 mg

Healthy Chocolate Mousse

Chocolate mousse is one decadent dessert that's loaded with tons of calories and sugar. It's a sinful treat that makes everyone happy. I decided to come up with a recipe that's as delicious and decadent as the original chocolate mousse but contains much healthier ingredients. This avocado mousse has agave syrup to sweeten it up, and the avocado itself will absorb the chocolate flavor so you won't notice its real taste, but a rich and satisfying flavor instead.

Prep time 5 minutes

Ingredients
1 ripe avocado, peeled and stoned
2 tablespoons cocoa powder
1½ tablespoons agave syrup
Pinch of salt
2 ounces dark chocolate, melted
½ teaspoon vanilla extract
5 raspberries for decoration

Directions
1. Place the avocado, cocoa powder, agave syrup, salt, vanilla, and melted chocolate in a food processor or blender.
2. Blitz until a smooth, thick mixture forms.
3. Pour in a glass and let it steep in the fridge for 30 minutes to set the chocolate.
4. Just before serving, decorate with fresh or frozen raspberries.

Nutrition (per serving)
Calories 889, fat 58.1 g, carbs 93.7 g, sugar 34.9 g
Protein 11.3 g, sodium 236 mg

Sweet Potato Parfait

If you love sweet potato, pumpkin, or apple pie, this sweet potato parfait is basically a pie in a glass. All you need is some time to make the sweet potato puree which will serve as a filling, and some delicious seeds and nuts to mix up to top this healthy dessert.

Prep time 10 minutes | Cooking time 15 minutes

Ingredients
1 small sweet potato, peeled
1 tablespoon agave syrup
¼ teaspoon vanilla extract
3 tablespoons coconut milk
Topping:
¼ cup rolled oats
2 tablespoons pecans, chopped
1 teaspoon sunflower seeds
1 teaspoon pumpkin seeds
1 teaspoon chia seeds
1 teaspoon agave syrup
¼ teaspoon cinnamon

Directions
1. Place the peeled sweet potato in a saucepan with water and bring to a boil. Cook for 15 minutes until tender.
2. Let cool completely and then puree until smooth.
3. Mix in the agave syrup, vanilla, and coconut milk.
4. In a small baking dish, place the rolled oats, chopped pecans, sunflower seeds, pumpkin seeds, chia seeds, and cinnamon.
5. Bake for 5 minutes in a preheated oven at 300°F (150°C).
6. Remove from oven. Mix in the agave syrup and toss.

7. Serve the sweet potato parfait with the baked granola on top.

Nutrition (per serving)
Calories 491, fat 28.3 g, carbs 54.8 g, sugar 6.3 g
Protein 9.7 g, sodium 47 mg

Insanely Good Blueberry Popsicles

Traditionally, fruit popsicles are made with pureed fruit and some sweetener, and they are frozen until they hold the shape. I am making a little twist by using frozen yogurt with blueberries and honey. The secret is in the lemon zest that goes so well with the blueberries.

Prep time 5 minutes | Cooling time 4 hours

Ingredients
3 ounces Greek yogurt
½ teaspoon vanilla extract
½ cup fresh blueberries
Zest of ½ lemon
1 tablespoon honey

Directions
1. Blitz the Greek yogurt in a food processor with the honey, vanilla, and lemon zest.
2. Stir in the fresh blueberries and transfer the mixture into a freezer-safe glass.
3. Place a stick in the center so you can remove the popsicle when needed.
4. Place in the freezer to set for around 4 hours.
5. When ready to eat, rinse the sides of the glass with warm water for 10 seconds so you can remove the popsicle easily.

Nutrition (per serving)
Calories 177, fat 2 g, carbs 31.8 g, sugar 28.2 g
Protein 9.2 g, sodium 30 mg

RECIPE INDEX

BREAKFAST — 5
    Overnight Oats — 5
    Breakfast Burrito — 6
    Banana Pancakes — 7
    Mushroom and Herb Omelet — 9
    Avocado Toast — 10
    Smoothie Bowl — 11

CHICKEN AND POULTRY — 13
    Primavera Stuffed Chicken — 13
    Perfectly Baked Chicken Breast — 14
    Air Fryer Chicken Breast Recipe — 15
    Lemon Garlic Baked Drumsticks — 16
    Creamy Tuscan Chicken — 17
    Turkey Meatballs — 18
    Turkey and Sweet Potato Casserole — 19
    Duck Breast with Orange Sauce — 21

BEEF, PORK, LAMB, AND VEAL — 23
    Pineapple Pork Stir Fry — 23
    Crisp Parmesan Pork Loin Steak — 25
    BBQ Meatballs — 27
    Veal Chops with Salsa — 29
    Veal Piccata — 31
    Greek-Style Lamb with Green Beans — 33
    Beef and Broccoli — 34
    Lamb Stuffed Zucchinis — 35

FISH AND SEAFOOD — 37
    Garlic Shrimp with Quinoa — 37
    Orange Salmon with Spinach Salad — 39
    Healthy Baked Salmon — 41
    Honey and Garlic Shrimp — 42

Shrimp Zoodles	43
Garlic Herbed Frilled Tuna Steak	45
VEGETARIAN	**47**
Caponata Pasta	47
Gnocchi with Mushrooms and Blue Cheese	49
Sweetcorn and Zucchini Fritters	51
Easy Vegetarian Quesadilla	51
Mushroom Bhaji	53
Coconut and Squash Curry	54
Veggie Fajita	54
Spinach and Ricotta Stuffed Shells	57
SNACKS AND SMALL BITES	**59**
Smoked Salmon Cucumber Bites	59
Greek Salad with Goat Cheese	61
Fresh Cherry Tomato Bruschetta	62
Peanut Butter Apple Slices	63
Dark Chocolate Bark with Almonds	64
Zucchini Baked Fries with Feta Cheese	65
Cheese Balls	67
Avocado Toast with Chia Seeds	68
Grilled Polenta	69
Chia Pudding with Three Ingredients	70
DESSERTS	**71**
Banana Pudding	71
Mini Donuts	73
Peanut Butter Mug Cake	75
Devil Chocolate Cake in a Mug	76
No-Bake Cookie Balls	77
Healthy Chocolate Mousse	78
Sweet Potato Parfait	79
Insanely Good Blueberry Popsicles	81

APPENDIX

Cooking Conversion Charts

1. Measuring Equivalent Chart

Type	Imperial	Imperial	Metric
Weight	1 dry oz.		28 g
	1 pound	16 dry oz.	0.45 kg
Vol-ume	1 tsp		5 ml
	1 dessert spoon	2 tsp	10 ml
	1 Tbsp	3 tsp	15 ml
	1 Australian Tbsp	4 tsp	20 ml
	1 fluid oz.	2 Tbsp	30 ml
	1 cup	16 Tbsp	240 ml
	1 cup	8 fluid oz.	240 ml
	1 pint	2 cups	470 ml
	1 quart	2 pints	0.95 l
	1 gallon	4 quarts	3.8 l
Length	1 inch		2.54 cm

* Numbers are rounded to the closest equivalent
Tsp = teaspoon
Tbsp = tablespoon
Oz. = ounce

2. Oven Temperature Equivalent Chart

Fahrenheit (°F)	Celsius (°C)	Gas Mark
220	100	
225	110	1/4
250	120	1/2
275	140	1
300	150	2
325	160	3
350	180	4
375	190	5
400	200	6
425	220	7
450	230	8
475	250	9
500	260	

* Celsius (°C) = T (°F)-32] * 5/9
** Fahrenheit (°F) = T (°C) * 9/5 + 32
*** Numbers are rounded to the closest equivalent

Printed in Great Britain
by Amazon